CW00879993

Other giftbooks by Helen Exley:
Klimt Notebook              Renoir Book of Days
Cézanne Notebook            Sunflowers A Birthday Book
Van Gogh Notebook           Van Gogh Diary 1999

Published simultaneously in 1997 by Exley Publications in Great Britain, and
Exley Giftbooks in the USA.

12  11  10  9  8  7  6  5  4  3  2  1

ISBN 1-85015-943-2

Pictures selected by Helen Exley.
Picture research by Image Select International.
Typeset by Delta, Watford.
Printed in China.
Astronomical and calendarial date is reproduced, with permission, from data supplied by HM
Nautical Almanac Office, © Particle Physics and Astronomy Research Council.
Exley Publications would like to thank the following organizations for permission to reproduce the
pictures and the border details in this book: Art Resource: cover, *Waterlilies: Green Reflections*,
Musée de l'Orangerie, Paris; endpapers: *Waterlilies, Morning (Version 1)*, Musée de l'Orangerie,
Paris; Edimedia: 28, 51; The Bridgeman Art Library: title page, *The Poppy Field*, 1873, Musée
d'Orsay, Paris, 19, 31, 41, 55, 67.

● NEW MOON     ○ FULL MOON

**Exley Publications Ltd, 16 Chalk Hill, Watford, Herts, WD1 4BN, UK.**
**Exley Giftbooks, 232 Madison Avenue, Suite 1206, NY 10016, USA.**

## *Claude Monet (1840-1926)*

*In 1872 Monet's painting Impression, Sunrise gave a new movement in art
its name: Impressionism. The Impressionists included Renoir and Cézanne,
and they worked in the open air, attempting to capture the fleeting
moment. Monet was a founder of this style of painting, and remained
faithful to its aims. Not an intellectual painter, he was, as his friend
Cézanne said, "merely an eye, but what an eye!". Monet developed a quick
spontaneous style to capture the ever-changing nuances of atmosphere and
light. He spent the last years of his life as a recluse at Giverny, where his
beautiful garden provided inspiration for his art.*

# 1 9 9 9
# MONET
## D I A R Y

**EXLEY**
NEW YORK • WATFORD, UK

# JANUARY

**1**    FRIDAY                                                      NEW YEAR'S DAY

**2**    SATURDAY    ○

**3**    SUNDAY

**4**    MONDAY

**5**    TUESDAY

**6**    WEDNESDAY

**7**    THURSDAY

*Branch of the Seine at Giverny*, 1896
Private Collection

# JANUARY

**8** FRIDAY

**9** SATURDAY

**10** SUNDAY

**11** MONDAY

**12** TUESDAY

**13** WEDNESDAY

**14** THURSDAY

FRIDAY *15*

SATURDAY *16*

● SUNDAY *17*

MONDAY *18*

TUESDAY *19*

WEDNESDAY *20*

THURSDAY *21*

# JANUARY

**22** FRIDAY

**23** SATURDAY

**24** SUNDAY

**25** MONDAY

**26** TUESDAY

**27** WEDNESDAY

**28** THURSDAY

*Mount Kolsass, Norway*, 1895
Private Collection

FRIDAY **29**

SATURDAY **30**

○ SUNDAY **31**

MONDAY **1**

TUESDAY **2**

WEDNESDAY **3**

THURSDAY **4**

FRIDAY **5**

SATURDAY **6**

SUNDAY **7**

*View of town across the river*
Private Collection

# FEBRUARY

**8** MONDAY

**9** TUESDAY

**10** WEDNESDAY

**11** THURSDAY

**12** FRIDAY

**13** SATURDAY

**14** SUNDAY                                    VALENTINE'S DAY

*View of Antibes*, 1888 (detail)
Private Collection

# FEBRUARY

**15** MONDAY

**16** TUESDAY ●                                              CHINESE NEW YEAR

**17** WEDNESDAY

**18** THURSDAY

**19** FRIDAY

**20** SATURDAY

**21** SUNDAY

MONDAY 22

TUESDAY 23

WEDNESDAY 24

THURSDAY 25

FRIDAY 26

SATURDAY 27

SUNDAY 28

# MARCH

**1** MONDAY

**2** TUESDAY ○

**3** WEDNESDAY

**4** THURSDAY

**5** FRIDAY

**6** SATURDAY

**7** SUNDAY

*Impression: Sunrise*, 1872
Musée Marmottan, Paris

## MARCH

**8**   MONDAY

**9**   TUESDAY

**10**   WEDNESDAY

**11**   THURSDAY

**12**   FRIDAY

**13**   SATURDAY

**14**   SUNDAY       MOTHER'S DAY (UK)

MONDAY *15*

TUESDAY *16*

● WEDNESDAY *17*

THURSDAY *18*

FRIDAY *19*

SATURDAY *20*

VERNAL EQUINOX                                                    SUNDAY *21*

**22** MONDAY

*Gare St. Lazare, 1877*
Musée d'Orsay, Paris

**23** TUESDAY

**24** WEDNESDAY

THURSDAY *25*

FRIDAY *26*

SATURDAY *27*

SUNDAY *28*

MONDAY *29*

TUESDAY *30*

○ WEDNESDAY *31*

# APRIL

**1** THURSDAY                                        PASSOVER

**2** FRIDAY                                          GOOD FRIDAY

**3** SATURDAY

**4** SUNDAY                                          EASTER DAY

**5** MONDAY                                          EASTER MONDAY

**6** TUESDAY

**7** WEDNESDAY

*Zuiderkerk, Amsterdam*, 1872 (detail)
Museum of Art, Philadelphia

# APRIL

**8** THURSDAY

**9** FRIDAY

**10** SATURDAY

**11** SUNDAY

**12** MONDAY

**13** TUESDAY

**14** WEDNESDAY

THURSDAY *15*

● FRIDAY *16*

ISLAMIC NEW YEAR                                    SATURDAY *17*

SUNDAY *18*

MONDAY *19*

TUESDAY *20*

WEDNESDAY *21*

**22** THURSDAY

*Through the trees of the Grande Jatte*
Private Collection

**23** FRIDAY

SATURDAY **24**

SUNDAY **25**

MONDAY **26**

TUESDAY **27**

WEDNESDAY **28**

THURSDAY **29**

○ FRIDAY **30**

# MAY

**1**   SATURDAY

**2**   SUNDAY

**3**   MONDAY

**4**   TUESDAY

**5**   WEDNESDAY

**6**   THURSDAY

**7**   FRIDAY

*Woman with Parasol, 1886*
Musée d'Orsay, Paris

# MAY

**8** SATURDAY

**9** SUNDAY                                          MOTHER'S DAY (US)

**10** MONDAY

**11** TUESDAY

**12** WEDNESDAY

**13** THURSDAY

**14** FRIDAY

● SATURDAY *15*

SUNDAY *16*

MONDAY *17*

TUESDAY *18*

WEDNESDAY *19*

THURSDAY *20*

FRIDAY *21*

## MAY

**22** SATURDAY

**23** SUNDAY

**24** MONDAY

**25** TUESDAY

**26** WEDNESDAY

**27** THURSDAY

**28** FRIDAY

*Tulip Field near Leiden, 1886*
The Hague

SATURDAY **29**

○    SUNDAY **30**

MONDAY **31**

TUESDAY **1**

WEDNESDAY **2**

THURSDAY **3**

FRIDAY **4**

SATURDAY **5**

SUNDAY **6**

MONDAY **7**

*Iris by the Pond*
Museum of Fine Arts, Richmond, Virginia

# JUNE

**8** TUESDAY

**9** WEDNESDAY

**10** THURSDAY

**11** FRIDAY

**12** SATURDAY

**13** SUNDAY ●

**14** MONDAY

JUNE

TUESDAY 15

WEDNESDAY 16

THURSDAY 17

FRIDAY 18

SATURDAY 19

FATHER'S DAY (US / UK)                                    SUNDAY 20

SUMMER SOLSTICE                                          MONDAY 21

# JUNE

**22** TUESDAY

**23** WEDNESDAY

**24** THURSDAY

**25** FRIDAY

**26** SATURDAY

**27** SUNDAY

**28** MONDAY   ○

*The Walk*
Christie's, London

# JULY

**1** THURSDAY

**2** FRIDAY

**3** SATURDAY

**4** SUNDAY

**5** MONDAY

**6** TUESDAY

**7** WEDNESDAY

*JULY*

THURSDAY *8*

FRIDAY *9*

SATURDAY *10*

SUNDAY *11*

MONDAY *12*

● TUESDAY *13*

WEDNESDAY *14*

# JULY

**15** THURSDAY

**16** FRIDAY

**17** SATURDAY

**18** SUNDAY

**19** MONDAY

**20** TUESDAY

**21** WEDNESDAY

*Pond at Argenteuil*
Museum of Art, Providence

# JULY

## 22 THURSDAY

## 23 FRIDAY

## 24 SATURDAY

*Zuiderkerk, Amsterdam*, 1872
Museum of Art, Philadelphia

SUNDAY **25**

MONDAY **26**

TUESDAY **27**

○ WEDNESDAY **28**

THURSDAY **29**

FRIDAY **30**

SATURDAY **31**

SUNDAY 1

MONDAY 2

TUESDAY 3

WEDNESDAY 4

THURSDAY 5

FRIDAY 6

SATURDAY 7

*Haysheaves*, 1887
Private Collection

# AUGUST

**8** SUNDAY

**9** MONDAY

**10** TUESDAY

**11** WEDNESDAY ● TOTAL ECLIPSE OF THE SUN

**12** THURSDAY

**13** FRIDAY

**14** SATURDAY

*Blanche Monet Painting*
Los Angeles County Museum

SUNDAY **15**

MONDAY **16**

TUESDAY **17**

# AUGUST

**18** WEDNESDAY

**19** THURSDAY

**20** FRIDAY

**21** SATURDAY

**22** SUNDAY

**23** MONDAY

**24** TUESDAY

WEDNESDAY 25

THURSDAY 26

FRIDAY 27

SATURDAY 28

SUNDAY 29

MONDAY 30

TUESDAY 31

# SEPTEMBER

**1** WEDNESDAY

**2** THURSDAY

**3** FRIDAY

**4** SATURDAY

**5** SUNDAY

**6** MONDAY

**7** TUESDAY

*Waterloo Bridge: Cloudy Weather,* 1900
Hugh Lane Gallery, Dublin

# SEPTEMBER

**8**    WEDNESDAY

**9**    THURSDAY    ●

**10**   FRIDAY

**11**   SATURDAY                             JEWISH NEW YEAR

**12**   SUNDAY

**13**   MONDAY

**14**   TUESDAY

*SEPTEMBER*

WEDNESDAY **15**

THURSDAY **16**

FRIDAY **17**

SATURDAY **18**

SUNDAY **19**

YOM KIPPUR

MONDAY **20**

TUESDAY **21**

# SEPTEMBER

**22** WEDNESDAY

**23** THURSDAY                                    AUTUMNAL EQUINOX

**24** FRIDAY

**25** SATURDAY ○

**26** SUNDAY

**27** MONDAY

**28** TUESDAY

*Waterlilies*, 1914
Portland Art Museum

FRIDAY **1**

SATURDAY **2**

SUNDAY **3**

MONDAY **4**

TUESDAY **5**

WEDNESDAY **6**

THURSDAY **7**

*Sailboats on the Seine*, 1874
Fine Arts Museum, San Francisco

# OCTOBER

**8** FRIDAY

*The Chailly Road, Fontainebleau, 1864*
Private Collection

**9** SATURDAY  ●

**10** SUNDAY

MONDAY **11**

TUESDAY **12**

WEDNESDAY **13**

THURSDAY **14**

FRIDAY **15**

SATURDAY **16**

SUNDAY **17**

# OCTOBER

**18** <sup>MONDAY</sup>

**19** <sup>TUESDAY</sup>

**20** <sup>WEDNESDAY</sup>

**21** <sup>THURSDAY</sup>

**22** <sup>FRIDAY</sup>

**23** <sup>SATURDAY</sup>

**24** <sup>SUNDAY</sup>  ○

OCTOBER

MONDAY **25**

TUESDAY **26**

WEDNESDAY **27**

THURSDAY **28**

FRIDAY **29**

SATURDAY **30**

SUNDAY **31**

# NOVEMBER

**1**    MONDAY

**2**    TUESDAY

**3**    WEDNESDAY

**4**    THURSDAY

**5**    FRIDAY

**6**    SATURDAY

**7**    SUNDAY

*Waterlily Pond*
National Gallery, London

# NOVEMBER

**8** MONDAY ●

**9** TUESDAY

**10** WEDNESDAY

**11** THURSDAY

**12** FRIDAY

**13** SATURDAY

**14** SUNDAY

MONDAY *15*

TUESDAY *16*

WEDNESDAY *17*

THURSDAY *18*

FRIDAY *19*

SATURDAY *20*

SUNDAY *21*

## 22 MONDAY

## 23 TUESDAY ○

*Pond with Waterlilies*
Private Collection

WEDNESDAY **24**

THURSDAY **25**

FRIDAY **26**

SATURDAY **27**

SUNDAY **28**

MONDAY **29**

TUESDAY **30**

WEDNESDAY 1

THURSDAY 2

FRIDAY 3

SATURDAY 4

SUNDAY 5

MONDAY 6

● TUESDAY 7

*Seascape*
Private Collection

## DECEMBER

**8** WEDNESDAY

**9** THURSDAY                                                FIRST DAY OF RAMADAN

**10** FRIDAY

**11** SATURDAY

**12** SUNDAY

**13** MONDAY

**14** TUESDAY

WEDNESDAY **15**

THURSDAY **16**

FRIDAY **17**

SATURDAY **18**

SUNDAY **19**

MONDAY **20**

TUESDAY **21**

# DECEMBER

**22** WEDNESDAY                                                WINTER SOLSTICE

---

**23** THURSDAY

---

**24** FRIDAY

---

**25** SATURDAY                                                  CHRISTMAS DAY

---

**26** SUNDAY                                                      BOXING DAY

---

**27** MONDAY

---

**28** TUESDAY

---

*DECEMBER*

WEDNESDAY **29**

THURSDAY **30**

NEW YEAR'S EVE

FRIDAY **31**

*Cliffs at Etretat*, 1868
Fogg Art Museum, Massachusetts